When Death is a Red Balloon

Poems by Linda Lerner

ISBN 9780999778463

First edition

Lummox Press
PO Box 5301
San Pedro, CA 90733
www.lummoxpress.com

Printed in the United States of America

ACKNOWLEDGMENTS

Grateful acknowledgment is made to the following journals in which these poems have appeared:

"Define it" and "Just Sand" appeared in *Piker Press*; "Every Sunday For Two Years" in *Trailer Park Quarterly;* "Autumnal" in the anthology *Before the Dawn* (Rogue Scholars Press, 2019); "Left Unfinished" in *Wilderness House Literary Review*; "Driving America" appeared in (*Takes Guts and Years Sometimes New and Selected Poems* (NYQ Books); "An Old Wives Tale or a Rip Van Winkle Story" first appeared in *Ding Dong the Bell Pussy in the Well (*Lummox Press)"Playing with Tense" accepted by *Gargoyle* for Summer 2020.

Parachute thoughts

I never once thought of a situation when I'd want a parachute. If my life depended on it, I'm sure I'd never be able to open it before crash landing somewhere. Even doing simple things, like trying to open a tightly fastened knot around my laundry bag is a struggle; I also lack the strength to open a tightly secured jar, and usually have to use pliers, and if that doesn't work, put it in hot water.

The absurdity is I've had a parachute for forty years without realizing it until he was gone.

Lowell was the person who made me feel that the possibility of a safe landing existed, a voice at the end of the phone to catch my fears, keep me from heading into dangerous worry-territory years ahead. When I got sick, was frightened, he was the first person I'd call. When something good happened, he was also the first person I'd tell.

He didn't always have a solution or rather, one that I'd accept. I had my own ideas. "You don't listen to me," he'd say, when what I did turned out to be a mistake. It sometimes did. I'm listening now, I'd tell him, if I could, wishing that I had, on a recent matter.

Out of habit, I check my answering machine for his voice, asking, are you all right, when I come home late at night; what sometimes annoyed me, I miss hearing now.

I've read accounts of people who've parachuted out of planes about to crash, and landed in a hard to reach place; some are eventually found, others not before it's too late.

There was a man whose parachute had become entangled and wouldn't open, who fell, 12,000ft. and survived that fall from 2.2 miles above Lake Taupo in New Zealand, with only a punctured lung and a broken ankle. "I should be dead, absolutely. I'd certainly given up hope," he said* but he's still alive. I think about that a lot, lately.

*info from The Daily Mail website 8/22/2018

CONTENTS

For Lowell Scheiner
12/26/33—7/2/2018

Every Sunday for Two Years

I asked if he wanted coffee and a bagel
or donut along with the NY Times
if he had enough milk
needed sugar, if he had
something for dinner that night
I asked about the book he was
working on with a man whose
grammar drove him crazy
if he wanted me to pick up
something at the post office
get him a book from Barnes & Noble
or a DVD he wanted to watch

I never asked if he needed something
he couldn't ask for

he never asked how I'd feel afterwards
not giving it to him

A leafy Sunday October Morning

it's a drizzly gray inside/out kind of day
doesn't really matter where I am
but better here to get through what
once was our day: the park, mostly
empty except for a few kids playing,
watchful parents close, a couple
with a dog seated on the next bench,
an elderly man walks back and forth
airing grievances I can't catch but
hear him clearly, moments of
other Sundays, quick flashes
as before a migraine a child's ball
breaks through, a parent's *sorry*
my *that's ok,* and for a few minutes is,
I bite into a bagel, let coffee break through
when a park attendant with a loud
leaf blowing machine sweeps
leaves into small groups to garbage
until the area is mostly cleared;
looks wrong, I think, emptied of
what life even dead leaves bring,
wrong, as when toward the end, he said,
"it almost doesn't seem worth it,"
a life gone with speed of light
into a single pronoun: wrong
to clear out everything

On Seeing Pinter's Old Times

I recall the wife talking about a college friend
she didn't like who stole her lingerie
and that incessant funereal music
that played over & over before the
play started, kept repeating the same thing,
Lowell said, seated three rows before me
reminding me that I'd seen the play
with him years ago which I didn't recall,
describing how beautiful the stage set was
in contrast to this dreary one; the music was
like a wall our words bounced off
and relieved when it finally stopped
the usher told me to get seated,
the theatre darkened, and the
play began… so tired, I kept forcing myself
to stay awake…last thing I heard
was the college friend singing a song,
then the cast members were taking bows
and the audience applauding a play
over when for me it had just begun;
I couldn't get past what happened,
face where it was leading me:
I don't understand, I kept repeating, as
we left the theatre and Pinter's Old Times
behind us

Left Unfinished

bad writing you'd say of
that seven-hour long sentence
you ran silently by me in the hospital,

a trick you had
to leave off writing in mid-sentence
for something to complete the next day,
worked you said
so I'm waiting
like a child who puts a tooth under her pillow
for the tooth fairy to get and leave
something in its place, I keep busy
sometimes grab a day
out of the wrong tense, lift a piece
of memory and play with the facts
to right a few wrongs

the grammarian & journalist would
not have approved, the man who
didn't know, just how much,
would have understood

Define It

Two women on skateboards are
heading straight toward me showing no
intention to change course or by their smiles
any desire to hit me which
a thank-you does, after I swerve
out of their way, *did it for me*
not you, I throw back in this fast moving
volley ball impromptu gone in
whip lashing bewilderment
                same time it took
for me to get that call from the hospital
that he was gone…I didn't say
I don't understand, that a month later
I still don't, because I get it. Only I don't

Being Lost

still daylight when you arrive
to get your hair cut, but night turns streets
around, hides signposts, and now can't
see which direction to go, walk
several blocks one way, then head
the opposite way several times
looking for your subway to get home---
it's that kind of lost you feel that
brought you here once before
without ever leaving where
you knew he'd always be
and no longer is

Just Sand

A woman is walking alone by the East River. I watch her from where I am sitting several feet away. Mid-July, a steamy month except for this fall like cool day. One of the ten best, someone I loved would have said. You'd agree. Hate hot weather... better than very cold, I always added —a running discourse we have. The woman is walking very slowly, one bag flung over her shoulder, another, larger one, over the other one. She notes two cops talking a few benches away, keeps them in her peripheral vision, and continues to walk at the same leisurely pace.

I am not fooled by this seeming calm, more like sleepwalking. She suddenly stops, looks across the river toward the World Trade Center, reaches into the larger bag, and flings out a handful of something over the railing before I can catch what it is. This happens a few more times.

The distance between us keeps growing shorter, though I haven't moved. She walks faster now as though diverted from what she hadn't planned on doing, and now late for something. It's such a perfect weather day. If I can find the right words, I'll bottle it for you to keep.

I don't know how long I've been sitting here, watching her, before she reaches her destination, stops and looks out at the Brooklyn Bridge except I am right there now; directly behind the bridge is the River Café. That's where you took me on my birthday. Remember? She digs into her bag and, like before, flings out a handful of something. Does it again. And again. A mother and child are standing nearby, watching her. "When my sister died," the mother said, "we scattered her ashes in Coney Island."

The boy turns around and says, "that's not ashes. It's just sand, Mommy." Now, indistinguishable from the woman's pixilated image breaking up over the East River.

I get up and start walking away. Maybe later, or tomorrow, I'll visit you.

Keeping Time

He had three other watches ticking off
his remaining time to remind him
but it's that watch I like to think of
keeping time in one of those jewelry stores
in Manhattan's west 40's, a Rolex
maybe Longines, ticking, like a heart
beating up to its last breath
ticket lost and he couldn't recall exactly where
kept good time, his heart beating strong,
the band stretched to its limits
his body headed in reverse, a '59 white convertible Ford
he could no longer drive speeding
back to 1980's "The Real Thing" * we shared
through March 2016, the curtain
coming down on O'Neil's Hughie."

*A play by Tom Stoppard

Driving America

a large white convertible cruises
into late December, turning heads,
a few rub their eyes, "wow, neat car,"
someone yells, another gives a thumbs-up
to the white-haired man behind the wheel;
he nods back,
just taking his baby out for a spin,
not wired to twenty first century sound-bytes
no seat belts to strap him in
It's 1959. His first car.
"aint nothin' but a hound dog" rocks;
just out of college and ready to make news
he's burning rubber in Brooklyn
the country still riding *I love Ike*
prosperity, victory in not
just one but future wars;

what would have paid
kids' college tuition, bought a nice home
keeps his engine running, heart beating:
50 years and good as new,
but every creak in the car's struggle
to push open its top echoes in his bones
means it's back to finding a mechanic
knows how to fix classic cars
won't rip him off;

price doesn't matter: in this car
he's lost nothing

driving down Flatbush Avenue toward
a sign that reads Atlantic
crosses another avenue back to
the mom & pop owned Brooklyn
of small grocery stores, drugstore counters
he sat at sipping egg creams, feeling
like he was standing in the outfield
at Ebbets Field ready to pitch into greatness,
back on that old route 66, reaching
skyward across the American imagination,
down streets barber shop poles twirl
red white and blue's possibilities;

people stop walking, stare
or peer out small car windows
from cost of gas, high rent & job worries
their own era's annihilation threats
roaring overhead to where
the Armageddon didn't happen
bomb the Russians never dropped,
stare at this shiny new-looking Ford
James Dean or Elvis might have driven
top pulled down waving to the crowd,
stare in wonderment; almost prayer...

two women in jeans, stiletto heels

rings in their noses, lips,

bring the troops home buttons on

jackets point to the car,

"it rocks" one shouts, he looks out,

abruptly rear ended by 2008;

"hey mister," the woman cries,

 "if you're going to Williamsburg,

can you give us a lift?"

Two Trips

  headed toward one place I didn't want to go to

when the plane lifted off for the other;

an hour ahead fell behind; when we landed

I wasn't sure which trip I was on

having prepared for southwest heat

not the other kind: my skin burning

in the 105°day's thoughts of

him, those tests he took, and fears

as I walked down San Antonio's streets

got lost & would learn that to lose

my way here is not really being lost.

find the Alamo, someone said, *and*

you'll know how to get back...I did

for nearly four decades, but how

to a place I don't recall being in

before someone who isn't my lover

and is more than a friend, who

pulled me back from edges I didn't even

know I was on...

I want out loud

to hear a voice so I can feel its words
breathing down on me, not
bloodless text conversations
so, when your voice escaped
through the copper cable wires of
last centuries hospital phone
I lit up: yours lost in the accident,
you complained, and about
the nurses, cardboard tasting food
uncomfortable bed, each complaint
leading me deeper into the word
back to the Caribbean Island
you visited as a young man
with your first ex, to the
golf course where you last
played with your late buddy
to a job you loved for over
20 years and without ever deviating
from that list of complaints,
your voice led me to the
edge of mortality's precipice

Back

A step forward sends him back to
a cane he no longer ignores
tries not to see the wheel chair
his mother & mine never got out of
behind it; gets another cane
he can fold up put back in that place
before he needed it, see his golf clubs
waiting by the door, mechanics' names
replacing doctors; someone who knows
about classic cars to tune up his
'59 white convertible he hasn't
driven for two years; *sell it* a new
young woman friend says

don't I tell this man I knew long before
the one I called husband, driving him
back into that car as he struggles
to get up from the coach,
won't let me help him; knows I am
not able to lift him up, that day

he called, feeling ill and I found him
lying on the floor in his office, helpless
to do anything but get a guard;
saw this man I've been leaning on for years
in time's backward spiral falling

away from me, unable to see

what another could do so easily:

get him back behind the wheel of his first car

heading off to the golf course, or a movie

his first woman beside him singing

along with Elvis…. the car rocking,

the convertible open, and sunlight

coursing through his soul

propelling him back into his future…

Autumnal

A corner fruit and vegetable store
I passed daily on my way home looked
the same as always, no sign of empty
wooden bins I'd see outside next day,
the store shuttered, *for good*, I asked someone,
for good he said; the wind whose autumnal
sound I'd shut my mind's ear to for years
picked up, reminded myself to be careful
avoid slipping on leaves plastering
sidewalks with their vegetable colors
taunting those admiring the bright
foliage, who paused, looking at the store
bewildered, who no longer thought
about that other one they'd spent hours
in among used books once overflowed
shelves a few blocks from where I live
not far from a pre-K school where
a variety mart once stood, *forever*
people said; that was before forever became
transitory when I could still smell him
reached out for his hand in bed every night
wasn't in mourning for another man
when this was still the same country
I was born in

Any proof?

A word breaks off from a question

when someone asked him, do you have any proof.

I laughed knowing what his answer would be

but when he added, "there's no proof of anything" *

it broke off from who said it

and like a dream fragment

wouldn't leave me alone, what can't be proved

in the aftermath of loss, what I know

as certain as I know I'm breathing

but no, I have no proof of what transpired

between us, no written record exists

only what I poem on paper

*A reference to when the president was asked if he had any proof there were Middle Eastern terrorists traveling in the caravan from Honduras to the U.S. border.

Gone

a big white dog materialized as I exited

the elevator onto your hallway floor,

transformed by the dimly lit space into a spectral being

held me in his gaze, pacing back and forth

outside his door seemed to be hovering

between two worlds as for weeks you had;

I don't know how long I stood watching that dog

watch me, only that he'd vanished when

hours later I left, having told you about it

said that he must belong to the people next door;

I never saw that dog again, or the person you

once were, and whom I knew would never see again

Seen from Afar

I watch him as from a planetary distance
this man I care for, quarrel with and
sometimes there's the word love, bumpy
like a street after a hard winter

he is looking down, slowly putting one foot
after another, people whiz by young
enough to be walking on the flat earth myth
he can't entirely let go of by using a cane

they do not see what I see, a man teetering
on its edge, that the edge is all there is now

a car whizzes by, feels like it is falling
out of the sky toward him, he grabs hold of
a young couple to steady himself...

"I'm ok now" he says, thanking them,
and stands up straight to show them
what he can't show me

An Old Wives Tale or A Rip Van Winkle Story

"step on a crack, you'll break your mother's back"
nothing about stepping over it, landing on the other side
stooped over in pain, the weight of over seven decades presses
down on you
"step on a line, you'll break your mother's spine"
she's long dead, it's your spine, came down
a curved genetic road to find you
after your father left, the man of the house;

cracks formed, the fine line between decisions
stepped over without consequences widened as
you walked the same pedestrian route habit mapped:
easiest distance between years: from home to work to the
same restaurant you and your mother once frequented

a struggle now to stand upright, you fight against
the downward gravitational pull of seventy plus years;
I do what I can, errands, simple tasks; not enough
the doctor gives you shots; it takes away the pain

you go back to who you were
and can never be again...

who's that old woman in the picture, my mother once asked
when I showed her a photo I took of her one day...

who's that man hunched over a cane I once couldn't

keep up with he walked so fast, who's that angry man

raging against injustice who reminds me of my father

....what happened to the one I've been leaning on all these years?

When Death Is a Red Balloon

Scared shitless last week when I
came to your room, saw you asleep
and kept calling your name
pulling your hand, *wake up*, I shouted
until you opened your eyes…

Oh, I tried again, sat by your bed for hours
holding your hand, sending my voice like a rope
to where you lay several levels below sleep

love, which never made it into word,
flowed through my touch with the meds from IV's
that kept you breathing

and then I saw that red balloon
like those in comics, instead of words,
a wire scrawl of hieroglyphics,
once there, wouldn't go away

I didn't want to see it hovering
near you, but I did; how you'd hate it,
It's not funny, you'd say, blaming me
for what I couldn't control

I watched the air slowly being let out.
Three hours passed and I left…it was just before…

the balloon is gone now

you are asleep, I am by your bedside

once again, holding your hand

if you can hear me, I must tell you

there is nothing I can ever imagine experiencing

more horrible than watching the air go out

of that balloon

On Hearing Your Friend Say,
You've Gone to a Better Place

When you heard someone said I should
give my sick cat "the gift of oblivion" anger sparked
at this clichéd attempt to be poetic about death

and when my cat against all odds revived
I could see it in your face,
you didn't have to say it, and when
you were in the hospital trying to decide
whether to have that life-saving operation
and the nurse said, "you don't look like
you're ready to die," and asked, "do you still
have things you want to do," you shook your head
yes and yes again, YES roared in my ears

and when after two days you hadn't woken up,
organs failing, and according to your wishes
not be kept breathing by artificial means,
machines about to be unplugged, I saw
your surgeon, in scrubs for another procedure,
quietly come in, her eyes searching
your chart for anything, "an interesting intelligent man"
she said of someone whose hard work to save you
super bugs sabotaged, found a 1% chance
you could...and so *could we wait just*
till this evening, yes, yes, YES I wanted to shout

— 24 —

only knew you wouldn't have approved of us arguing

but I know with absolute certainty, and
knowing it probably wouldn't have
made a difference, if it was your friend or me,
you would have waited

Playing with Tense

(written immediately on waking, 4/7/2019)

It's early April; I'm telling him about
a play I saw in the fall, *The Lifespan of a Fact*,
I thought he would have liked.
Maybe they'll revive it, I say, though
it's not likely, but...He looks hopeful.
I am too. There's more color in his face, and
he seems strong enough and ready
to get out of his wheelchair, to continue
from where he was a few years ago.
The weather is getting warmer;
maybe he'll be able to go down
to the Brooklyn Heights promenade
where we often liked to walk.
I don't bring up the business of those ashes
I threw into the East river in July.
It has nothing to do with him. He
agrees. I just focus on the present,
now that he got better from death.

Bio

Linda Lerner's last collection, *A Dance Around the Cauldron,* a prose work which consists of nine characters during the Salem witch trials brought into modern times. (Lummox Press, September, 2017.) was nominated for a Pushcart prize. *Yes, the Ducks Were Real*, was published by *NYQ Books* (2015) as was her previous full- length collection, *Takes Guts and Years Sometimes.* In addition to poetry, she's published essays, short prose and book reviews in magazines throughout the country. *In 2015* she read six poems on WBAI for Arts Express;

In 1995 she and Andrew Gettler began *Poets on the Line,* (http://www. echony.com/~poets) the first poetry anthology on the Net for which she received two grants. Andrew was a Nam Vet, who turned against the war, as did many of the poets included in this issue. They were part of a group who threw their medals into the White House Lawn.

"Taking the F Train" is forthcoming from NYQ Books.

The **LUMMOX Press** was established in 1994
and published the Little Red Book series and
the Lummox Journal. It now publishes
chapbooks, a perfect bound book series,
a Poetry Anthology & Poetry Contest
(annually), and "e-copies" (PDFs) of
many of the perfect bound titles.

The goal of the press is to elevate
the bar for poetry, while bringing
the "word" to an international audience.
I am proud to offer this book
as part of that effort.

For more information and to see our
growing catalog of choices, please go to
www.lummoxpress.com